AUSTRALIA'S REMARKABLE WILDLIFE

JOHN LESLEY

ECHIDNA

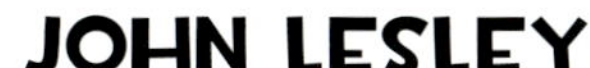

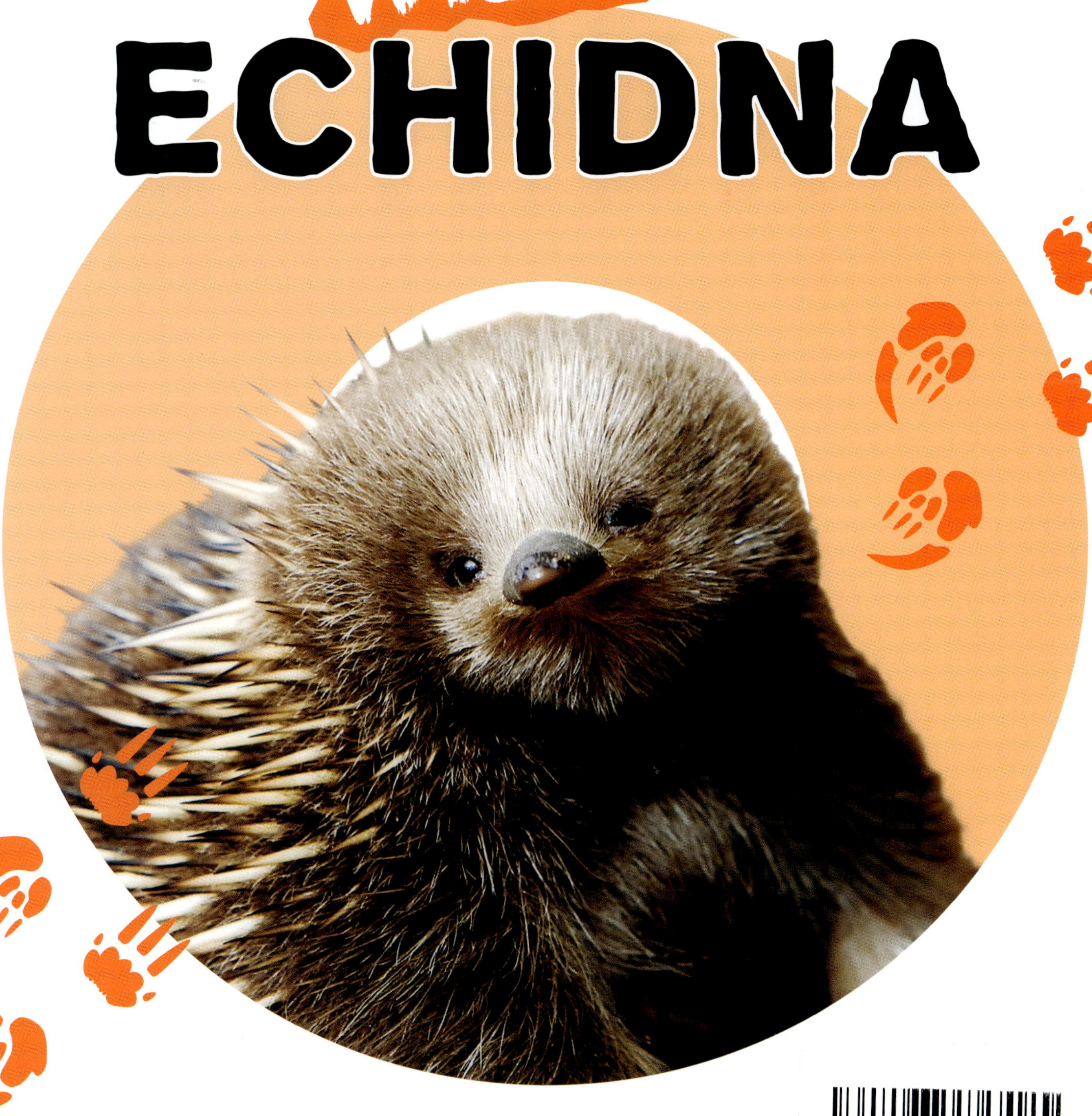

REDBACK publishing

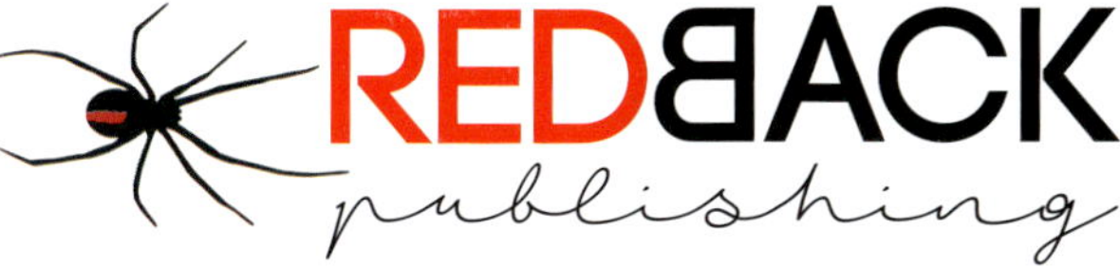

First Published 2025 by
Redback Publishing
Suite 6, 13a Narabang Way,
Belrose NSW 2085
Australia

www.redbackpublishing.com
orders@redbackpublishing.com

ISBN 978-1-761400-19-3 PBK

Author: John Lesley
Editor: Caroline Thomas
Design: Redback Publishing

A catalogue record for this book is available from the National Library of Australia

Original illustrations © Redback Publishing 2025
Originated by Redback Publishing

Printed and bound in Malaysia

Acknowledgements
Abbreviations: l—left, r—right, b—bottom, t—top, c—centre, m—middle
We would like to thank the following for permission to reproduce photographs: (Images © shutterstock)
p21tr User:Jaganath, CC BY-SA 3.0 (http://creativecommons.org/licenses/by-sa/3.0/), via Wikimedia Commons, p24-25c Harley Kingston, p30tr Helgen KM, Portela Miguez R, Kohen J, Helgen L, CC BY 3.0 (https://creativecommons.org/licenses/by/3.0), via Wikimedia Commons

CONTENTS

WHAT IS AN ECHIDNA?

Many people think of echidnas as Australia's version of the European hedgehog or the American porcupine. All three animals have developed sharp spines on their backs to protect themselves, but that is where the similarity ends. Porcupines are rodents, related to rats and guinea pigs. They are herbivores and eat plants. Hedgehogs are related to shrews and moles, and they eat insects and worms.

Giant anteater pictured in Brazil

As a further way to try to understand what the echidna is, people have also compared it to the anteaters of South America by calling it a spiny anteater. Despite all these attempts to find an existing group of animals that the echidna could join, we now know that the echidna is unique and not closely related to any other animals in the world, except for the platypus.

Species	Echidnas	Hedgehog	Porcupine
Continent	Australia (including New Guinea)	Africa, Asia, Europe	South America
Food	Carnivore (mostly ants)	Carnivore (insects and worms)	Herbivore (seeds, grass, bark, leaves)
Type of Mammal	Monotreme (related to the platypus)	Placental (related to shrews and moles)	Placental (rodent)
Spines	Yes	Yes	Yes
Lays Eggs	Yes	No	No

MONOTREMES

Both echidnas and platypuses are the only two examples left alive on Earth of the rare group of mammals called monotremes. Echidnas only live in Australia and New Guinea, and platypuses are only in Australia.

Monotremes are a very ancient type of mammal, and they have one surprising feature. They all lay eggs!

TYPE OF ANIMAL

The echidna is a monotreme mammal, which means it has these characteristics:

- The adults are covered in fur
- The female lays eggs
- The echidna feeds its babies on milk from the mother's body

The echidna and platypus both have the lowest body temperatures of any mammal that is not hibernating. This is because they cannot control their temperature the way marsupials and placental mammals do, suggesting a connection with very distant reptilian ancestors which are 'cold-blooded'.

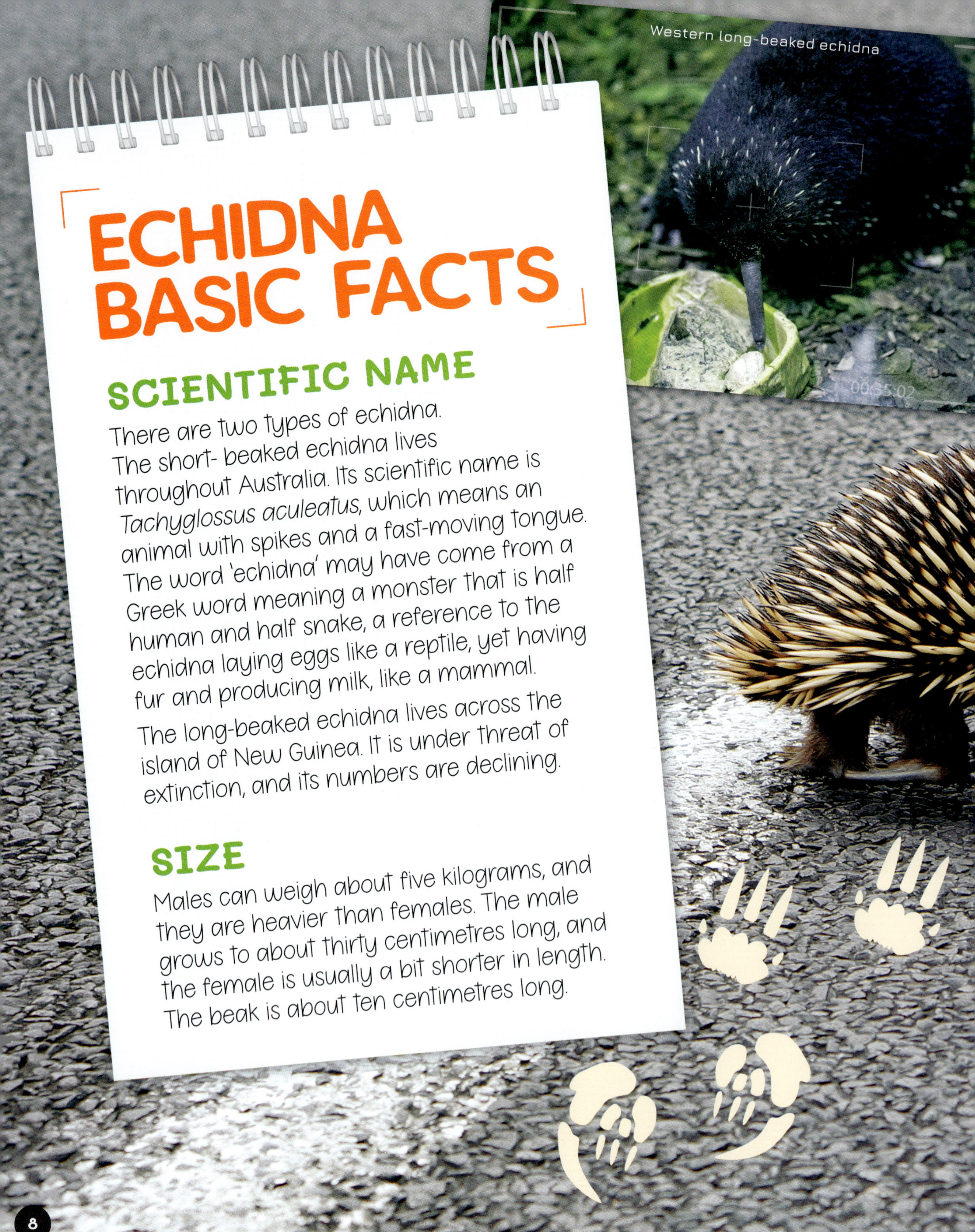

ECHIDNA BASIC FACTS

SCIENTIFIC NAME

There are two types of echidna. The short- beaked echidna lives throughout Australia. Its scientific name is *Tachyglossus aculeatus*, which means an animal with spikes and a fast-moving tongue. The word 'echidna' may have come from a Greek word meaning a monster that is half human and half snake, a reference to the echidna laying eggs like a reptile, yet having fur and producing milk, like a mammal.

The long-beaked echidna lives across the island of New Guinea. It is under threat of extinction, and its numbers are declining.

SIZE

Males can weigh about five kilograms, and they are heavier than females. The male grows to about thirty centimetres long, and the female is usually a bit shorter in length. The beak is about ten centimetres long.

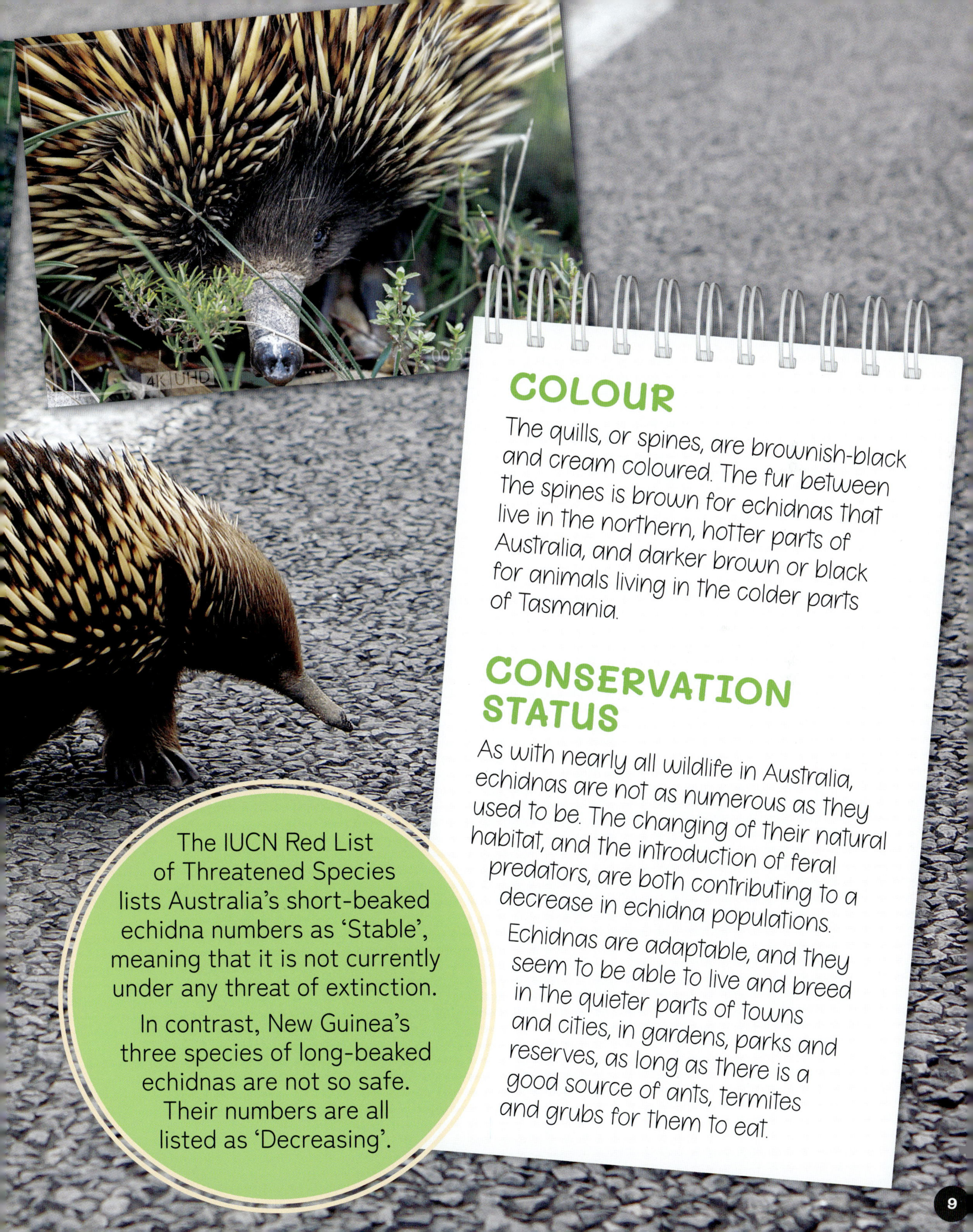

COLOUR

The quills, or spines, are brownish-black and cream coloured. The fur between the spines is brown for echidnas that live in the northern, hotter parts of Australia, and darker brown or black for animals living in the colder parts of Tasmania.

CONSERVATION STATUS

As with nearly all wildlife in Australia, echidnas are not as numerous as they used to be. The changing of their natural habitat, and the introduction of feral predators, are both contributing to a decrease in echidna populations.

Echidnas are adaptable, and they seem to be able to live and breed in the quieter parts of towns and cities, in gardens, parks and reserves, as long as there is a good source of ants, termites and grubs for them to eat.

The IUCN Red List of Threatened Species lists Australia's short-beaked echidna numbers as 'Stable', meaning that it is not currently under any threat of extinction.

In contrast, New Guinea's three species of long-beaked echidnas are not so safe. Their numbers are all listed as 'Decreasing'.

THE ECHIDNA BODY

ADAPTATIONS

An adaptation can be either a change in the body, or a new type of behaviour that animals have developed to allow them to survive better in their environment.

An adaptation can be the result of a change in the animal's DNA in its genes, producing some helpful feature. This change can then be passed to their offspring.

When an animal learns a new behaviour that makes it more successful, it then needs to pass this behaviour to its offspring through learning rather than by inheritance through its DNA and genes.

LONG TONGUE

The sticky, long tongue gets into the crevices of termite and ant nests, where it collects the insects and then carries them back into the mouth.

NOSTRILS

These are located on the top of the tip of the beak, allowing the echidna to breathe when it is swimming.

TUBE-LIKE SNOUT OR BEAK

The beak has electroreceptors that allow an echidna to pick up information about ants and insects in the ground. The mouth is very small and right at the end of the tube. This adaptation is perfect for eating ants, but it restricts the size of food that an echidna could get into its mouth.

FRONT CLAWS

The front claws are very strong for digging burrows, for tearing apart rotting wood and for getting to food under the ground.

SHARP SPINES

The spines, or quills, protect an echidna from being eaten by most wild predators. Although they are very strong and sharp, the spines are made from keratin, the same substance that vertebrate animal bodies use to make nails and hair.

WADDLING WALK

The waddling walk of the echidna is a result of the limbs sticking out sideways from the body, rather than pointing downwards. This feature is similar to the way limbs are attached to the body in reptiles, and reveals that echidnas are an ancient type of mammal.

THICK FUR

In cold regions, thick fur grows between the spines to keep the echidna warm.

HIND CLAWS

These are facing backwards, which makes digging a quick hole in the ground easier when they are trying to escape a predator. The shape of these claws is adapted for grooming the fur between the spines.

Echidnas can be infested with one of the biggest fleas that exists, and grooming the fur to get rid of these is important for the echidna's general health.

ARE THEY POISONOUS?

Echidna spines do not have poison on them, but an injury from a spine can become infected. The spines are large and sharp enough to inflict a very unpleasant wound on any person or animal that gets too near to an echidna.

SPURS

Like the platypus, the echidna male has a sharp spur on its hind legs. In the platypus, this spur is connected to a venom gland, but in the echidna no venom is produced. The gland's role seems to be to produce a scent that is used for communication with other echidnas.

PROTECTION

If it is caught in a place where it cannot burrow, an echidna will roll itself into a ball, protecting its soft belly and face and making the spines all stick straight outwards.

SHY AND SHARP

Echidnas are shy and will not attack with their spines. They will try to burrow into the ground, leaving the sharp spines sticking up out of the dirt, ready to impale a hand, foot or claw.

Echidnas do not release their spines into a predator like porcupines do.

ECHIDNA HABITATS

REGIONS

Echidnas are found throughout Australia. They live in the arid, semi-desert regions, in forests and grasslands, in cold, alpine areas and even in suburban backyards. In hot areas, echidnas escape the heat by hiding in a burrow or hollow log, and then only coming out to forage in the evenings or early morning.

TORPOR IN THE COLD

In cold regions, echidnas enter a state of torpor, or part hibernation. They snuggle into their burrow and go to sleep until the worst of the winter is over. Hibernation and torpor both allow an animal to survive for long periods without having to eat or drink.

BURROWS

Echidnas live in burrows that they dig for themselves, or that they find abandoned by wombats or other burrow-living creatures. An echidna may also choose to live inside a hollow log, under rocks, or hidden amongst rubbish in a garden.

ECHIDNA LIFE CYCLE

Echidnas are solitary animals, only being in the company of others to mate or to raise their young.

MATING

Mating between the male and female echidna results in the female laying one, very small egg a few days later. She moves the egg into the pouch that has developed on the outside of her body. The egg has a soft shell, like those of reptiles, and is less than two centimetres long.

4K UHD

LIFESPAN

Puggles gradually start to claim their own territory and live alone until they are ready to mate. Echidnas may live for around fifteen years.

HATCHING

The baby has a special, sharp tool on its beak that helps it to break out of the egg. This is also the way that baby reptiles hatch out of their shells.

PUGGLES

The baby echidna is called a puggle. It has no spines, it is hairless and blind, and it feeds on milk that the mother produces from patches in the pouch.

LEAVING THE BURROW

After a few weeks, the puggle starts to grow spines, and this is the cue for the mother to build a nursery burrow for it and expel it from her pouch. The puggle stays in the burrow, and the mother returns every few days to feed it milk. The puggle is old enough to leave the burrow and look after itself after about seven months.

Puggle

ECHIDNA ANCESTORS

60 MILLION YEARS AGO

The echidna and platypus both descend from a single ancestor that lived about sixty million years ago. This is around the time that a meteor fell to Earth and probably resulted in the destruction of the dinosaurs.

An outcome of this terrible event was that the small mammals alive at the same time as dinosaurs then had a better chance of spreading and evolving into the thousands of mammal species that are alive today, as well as those that have become extinct in the past sixty million years.

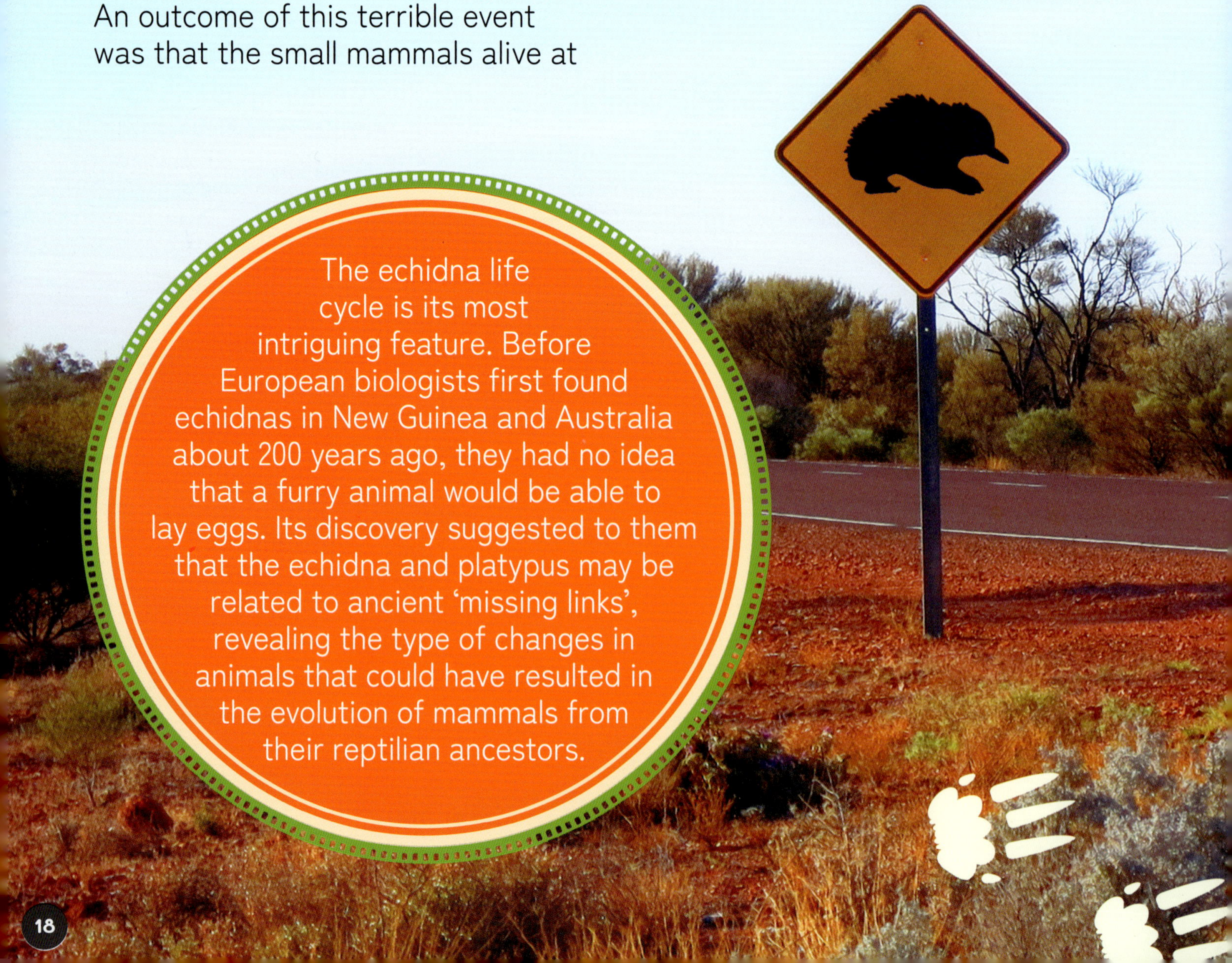

The echidna life cycle is its most intriguing feature. Before European biologists first found echidnas in New Guinea and Australia about 200 years ago, they had no idea that a furry animal would be able to lay eggs. Its discovery suggested to them that the echidna and platypus may be related to ancient 'missing links', revealing the type of changes in animals that could have resulted in the evolution of mammals from their reptilian ancestors.

10,000 YEARS AGO

Before ten thousand years ago, Australia, Tasmania, New Guinea and most of the islands between them were all one mass of land. Sea levels were lower than they are today, and this allowed animals to move between areas that are now isolated from each other by seas and oceans, but which were then dry land.

Short and long-beaked echidnas lived across the whole region. As ice at the Poles melted around ten thousand years ago, the sea levels rose. This resulted in animals becoming isolated from each other as water surrounded Australia, and separated Tasmania. Echidnas then changed through evolution into the types that are now found on each island and landmass.

WHAT ECHIDNAS EAT

The short-beaked echidna that lives in Australia is a carnivore. It is specialised to eat ants and termites, grabbing them with its sticky tongue and sucking them up through its long mouth. It does not have any teeth, but it does have hardened areas in its mouth that it can use to squash soft insects before swallowing them.

The long-beaked echidna in New Guinea prefers to eat worms and grubs.

THREATS TO ECHIDNAS

Echidnas prefer to hide from people and other animals, so they are not often seen in the wild, which is one reason why they have survived so well.

HABITAT

Destruction of the echidna's natural habitat has driven some of them to seek refuge in gardens. While they can often survive there if they are not disturbed, their breeding will be disrupted. Echidnas only produce one egg per year, and the puggle is very vulnerable for many months.

PREDATORS

Feral and native animals are a threat to echidnas. Snakes and goannas enter burrows and eat the puggles before the spines have developed enough to protect them.

Feral and domestic dogs and cats, as well as foxes and dingoes, all try to eat echidnas. They can dig up a puggle's burrow and kill it, but feral animals are so clever that many of them have also learned how to attack an adult echidna without getting injured by the spines. Some dogs know how to turn an echidna over and attack its belly where there are no spines.

PROTECTED

Echidnas are protected animals throughout Australia. This means they must not be harmed, moved or kept as pets. People who find an injured echidna should contact local wildlife services. If an echidna is picked up and then slips to the ground, its long beak can be easily damaged. A sick echidna may still be able to use its extremely strong claws.

PEOPLE AND ECHIDNAS

CLIMATE CHANGE

Climate change is contributing to rising summer temperatures, and what appears to be an increase in the number and severity of weather events such as flooding, droughts and storms. All these factors contribute to dangerous changes to the habitat and environment that echidnas need to survive and breed each year.

HUMAN ACTIVITIES

The human population of Australia is growing all the time. People need more space for their homes, roads and towns, and this means that less natural space is left for wildlife. Even in natural bushland, cars on roads pose a threat to echidnas. Mining and logging also take land away from native wildlife.

WHERE TO SEE ECHIDNAS

ZOOS

Zoos and wildlife parks in Australia nearly all have echidnas amongst their animal inhabitants. Echidnas do not often breed in captivity, so keeping a population of echidnas in a zoo is often a challenge for the zookeepers.

IN A GARDEN

If you live near the bush, do things to make your garden echidna-friendly. Don't use insecticides, as these will kill the ants and termites that the echidna is looking for. Provide places where the echidnas can burrow and hide, such as hollow logs, and don't let a dog in the area where you hope to see an echidna.

Echidnas like to hide in all the leaves and dead branches on the ground that are found in a natural forest area. Unfortunately, this is exactly the type of litter that homeowners are told to remove from their properties to lessen the risk of damage from bushfires. Reconciling the needs of people with those of echidnas is a very difficult task.

IN THE WILD

To see a wild echidna in the bush, you need to be very patient, quiet and lucky. An echidna will hear and smell you coming and will hide until you go away. If you want to see wildlife in the bush, never take your dog with you. Wild animals hate dogs and can smell them long before they arrive and long after they leave an area.

4K UHD 3...2...1...0...1...2...3 00:35:02

SORTING ANIMALS INTO GROUPS

Biologists divide all living things around the world into groups. They call this process classification.

Here are the basic groups that describe all animals with backbones:

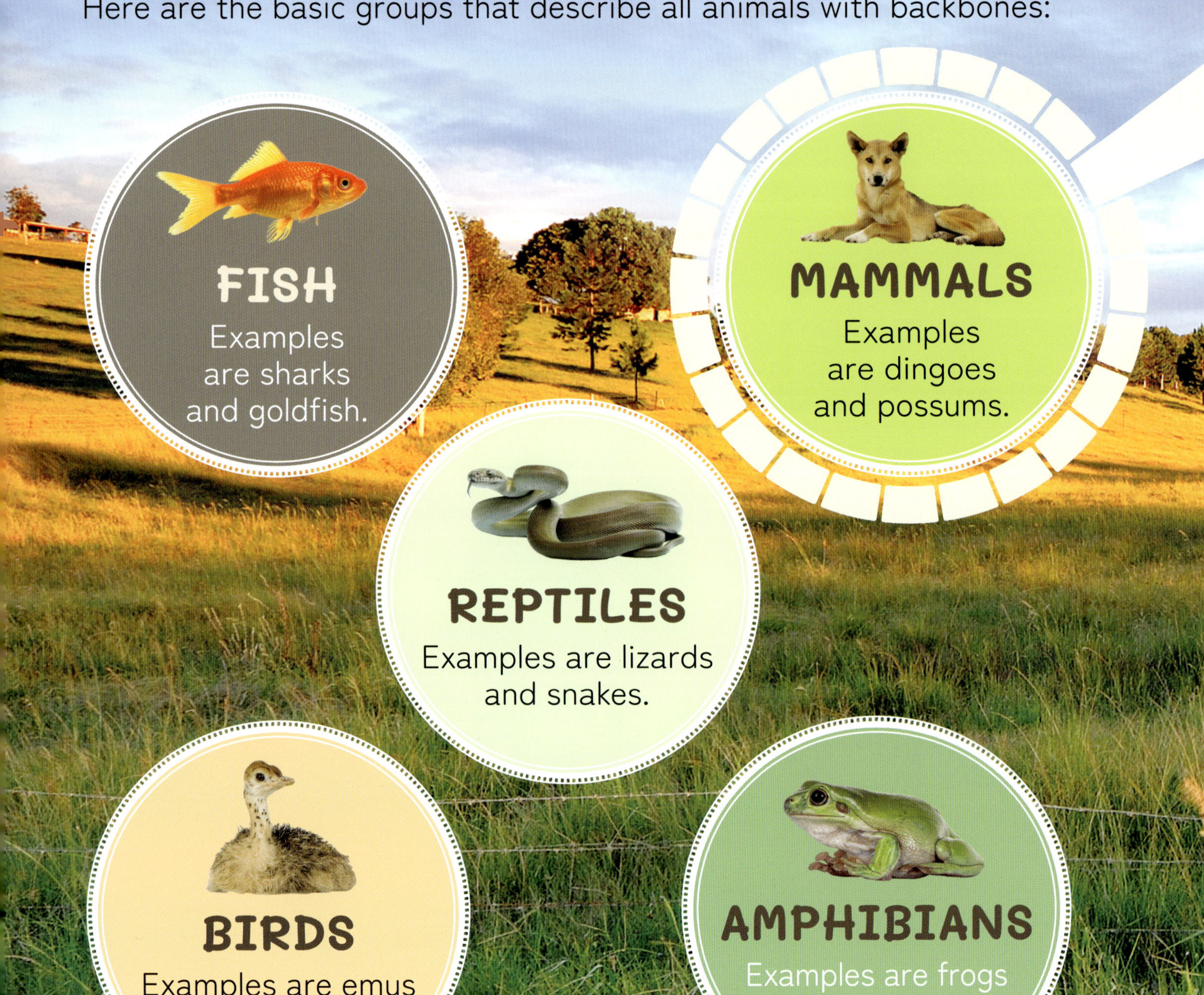

Mammals are further divided into three main groups:

MONOTREME MAMMALS
Examples are echidnas and platypuses.

PLACENTAL MAMMALS
Examples are whales and humans.

MARSUPIAL MAMMALS
Examples are kangaroos and koalas.

HOMO SAPIENS

Humans have a scientific name and a position in the classification of animals. We are called *Homo sapiens*. These Latin words mean 'smart person'.

THE FUTURE OF ECHIDNAS

Echidnas have been in Australia for millions of years. Indigenous Australian rock art from thousands of years ago shows the echidna as an important source of food. The early European settlers also tried eating echidnas.

Aboriginal rock art depicting an echidna

The echidna and the platypus are the only two examples of egg-laying mammals left alive on Earth, making them both extremely precious. Echidnas don't breed well in captivity, which makes captive breeding programs less successful than they have been with other rare animals, like the giant panda or the Tasmanian devil.

In the future, the main threats to the continued existence of this very special little animal will be the loss of habitat through humans needing more land for themselves, and through the ongoing effects of climate change.

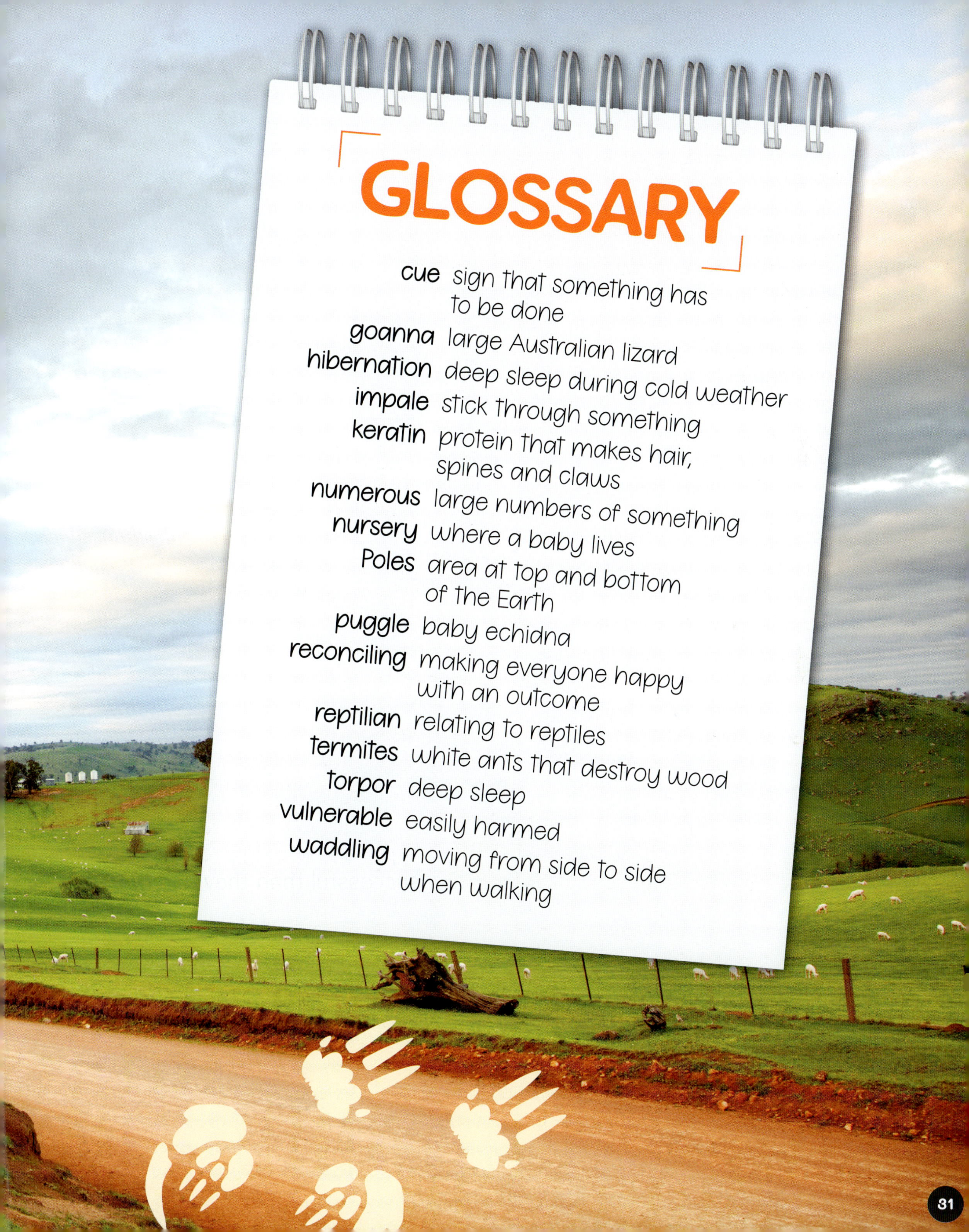

GLOSSARY

cue sign that something has to be done

goanna large Australian lizard

hibernation deep sleep during cold weather

impale stick through something

keratin protein that makes hair, spines and claws

numerous large numbers of something

nursery where a baby lives

Poles area at top and bottom of the Earth

puggle baby echidna

reconciling making everyone happy with an outcome

reptilian relating to reptiles

termites white ants that destroy wood

torpor deep sleep

vulnerable easily harmed

waddling moving from side to side when walking

INDEX